Soul Song

Sandra Boston

© 2015 Sandra Boston
All rights reserved

978-0-9969719-3-5

Photography by Sandra Boston
Book design Maureen Moore
Ginger Cat's Booksmyth Press
www.thebooksmythpress@gmail.com

Dedication

I dedicate this collection of my soul songs to the teachers who have midwifed my willingness to write, Pam Roberts, Julie Payne Britton, Nancy Slonim Aronie, Marge Piercy, Patricia Lewis, and Mary Clare Powell. Each has disciplined me as only the best teachers will; they taught me to trust what comes, let the muse lead and find its own outcome.

And I dedicate these songs to all those who crossed my path and whose spirits dance through these pages and make my heart so happy.

Acknowledgments

I am deeply grateful to my readers, Mary Clare Powell and Gaella Elwell who took pen to paper and weeded like gardeners to bring forth a better harvest of words, sentiment and clarity.

I am also grateful to my writing partners, Cheryl Fox and Allie Taylor who listened, danced with my muse, and enhanced my perspective.

Come, come, whoever you are.
Wanderer, worshiper, lover of leaving.
It doesn't matter.
Ours is not a caravan of despair.
Come, even if you have broken your vows
a thousand times.
Come, yet again, come, come.
— Jelaluddin Rumi

What the soul needs
more than anything
is time when we are doing
nothing.
—Thomas Moore, *Care of the Soul*

Contents

Acknowledgments   3
Introduction   11

1 To Cherish My Experience and Harvest Life's Wisdom

Crone   17
Clearing   18
Circle   19
With Neither Haste Nor Regret   20
Warrior Woman   21
What if Life …   23
I Feel Love in My Bones   25
The Door Opens   27
The Great Nap   28
Am I Lost?   31
Reunion   33

2 To Savor My Wanderings and Musings

Invitation   37
Bend Down   38
God Nectar   39
Mystery   40
The Altar of Beauty   41
Parade   42
Open Heart   43
God is in My Garden   44
If Mother Nature is Family   45
Spring's Arising   47

Dark Spark   48
Sing a Song of Summer   49
Come Silence   50
Welcome Bodhi   51
I Know I Am Home   53

3 To Be Surprised by Wit, Humor, and Life Laughing at Itself

Why Not Fly?   57
Max   59
Lorraine   61
My Grandmother is a Bag Lady   64

4 To Pray through My Pen, from Soul to Source

God of This Crystal-Clear Morning   73
Transition   74
Praise   75
King David's 23rd Psalm to the Great Mother   77
My Birthday Prayer   78
Clearing the Deck   80
Grandchild A-Borning   81
Be the Way   85
Winter Solstice   86

5 To Redeem a Loss or Hurt and to Search for Redemption

Hear the Earth Crying   91
What is Being Taken?   92
Four Millimeters   94
Mystery of Belonging   96
Hearts See   97
The Altar of Kindness   98

Still I Sing   99
Honey Pot   100
Wait a Minute   101
War Rant   102
The Spoiler   106
Oh Say Can You See   108
Spiritual Resilience   109
Lost Dreams of Easy Times   111
Mom   112
Empty Nest   113
Love Embraces Us   114
Recovery   115
Give the World to the Women   116

6 To Listen for the Guidance of Spirit

Communion   121
Living into Love   122
In the Heart of Spirit   123
Pilgrim   125
When Change Comes   126
Stopping to Hug a Tree   128
I Am the Love Already with You   130
Got Soul?   131
How Many?   132
How Do I Know God?   133
Labyrinth   134

7 To Bow in Thanksgiving for My Life

We are All One   141
Bestowing Blessing   142
Duet of Praise   143
Ego and Soul Say Goodbye   144
I Greet Spirit   146
Grandmother Sandra   147

Introduction
Why Do I Write?

Writing, for me, is an act of devotion—a coming to the altar of life with a grateful and open heart. My arrival creates sacred space. Such devotion turns the act of writing into a song of the soul. I come singing for the joy of communing with my soul and my muse—are they the same? I come in wonder. I come, watching for the space between words where ideas and phrases take form. I come to attend a birth.

Sometimes, I come like the mother who must get up in the middle of the night to tend a frightened child. The mother's devotion matches the intensity of the child's wail. I come to writing as if I am responding to a wail within me. It is a wail for meaning—for naming and responding to my teachers, and the strangers both animate and inanimate who cross my path and leave me changed. I come, willing to trust the leading of soul, and be surprised by what arises. I come to worship rather than to own.

I come searching for the hidden jewels—the realizations that come in hindsight after a storm has passed, or something precious has been lost, or something unexpected has been given. I bring devotion to each jewel. I ponder the impulse behind the giving or the finding. Where do these messages come from?

I come to play, too. It's fun to follow an idea and see where it wants to go. It's exciting to create a story that finds its own ending. I walk on sacred ground when I revisit precious moments with special people. It's healing to find, in the recounting of a wounding, forgiveness that wasn't there before. Such experiences are a living, breathing blessing from beyond that opens me to a bigger vista, a bigger self, and a bigger circle of shared meanings. Writing with devotion calls me forth, showers me with grace, and fills my days with mystery and delight. I hear my soul song.

The section titles that shape the journey through these pages come from the prompt: Why do I write?

To Cherish My Experience and Harvest Life's Wisdom

Crone

Alive to life
Aware of presence
On the move
Praying for acceptance
Saying "yes" more than "no"
Gratitude, gratitude, gratitude
Following my bliss, my purpose, my guidance
Journeying inward to soul,
Outward to grace
Singing my soul song
Sharing power, vision, inspiration
Watching for the dawn
Marching for justice
Seeking peace within and without
Shouting hallelujah to the spring
Meeting my fear and befriending it
Welcoming love, radiating love
Cherishing solitude, stillness
Swinging in the hammock
Passing the torch
Beginning again
Watching grandchildren grown
Tending the garden
Living freedom
Traveling to foreign lands
Listening to the muse
Awakening the writer
Celebrating beauty
Allowing time its due
Searching the heavens for home
Being home
Breathing now.

Clearing

Quiet…Still…Alone…Secluded,
Conscious of choice,
I surrender,
Allowing life to unfold.
Halt to plans, connections, responsibilities,
Free fall…flight…wings….drift…soar,
Surprise…
"I am happy with you," the Grandmother blesses me.
"You are never alone. You dance in my heart.
Someday the path ahead will open out and dissolve
Into the Sea of Existence
Where there is only memory, pure awareness,
No ego, no past-present-future,
Just is-ness, released from earth's hold.
So relish life, each plant, flower, seed, creature,
Spring rain,
Each gift from a friend,
Each meal a gift from earth and sun,
Each song an anthem of existence.
Let the melodies play up your spine.
Feel your body alive, happy, open.
Let worries be washed clean by the tide.
Utter thanks for the beauty of it all.
Open."

Circle

Circle, circle, circle,
More power in a circle,
More calm in a circle,
More arms to hold the pain,
More voices to raise the prayer,
More breath to blow on the embers of hope
       after the holocaust of hate.

More eyes to see what is being revealed,
More hands to do the work of rebuilding trust
       in the goodness of humankind.

More songs to sing the soul of the earth
       to weary spirits,
More silence to wait patiently
       for renewal and guidance.

More balance to urge the disconnected,
       and restrain the urgent,
More humility to sit with the unanswered question
       of "Why?"

More wisdom to turn over the as yet unturned stone
       for understanding,
More patience to learn from the lessons of pain and loss.

More broken hearts to open to forgiveness,

More resilience to feel again the gift of the Circle,

More of being alive together as One.

With Neither Haste Nor Regret

With neither haste nor regret, I move toward Source. What do I mean by Source?

Source is a pulsing energy of pure Being without name or story.

Source is the reality surrounding and holding all our impatience to know the truth, our need to make up stories to solve the mystery of where life comes from and where it goes when the body that was vibrant is now cold and gray.

Source sings hallelujah through birdsong, frog croak, dog bark, human aria or poem, and the artist's masterpiece.

Source announces its presence in the sunrise and sunset, the starling crack of thunder and streak of lightening.

Source sings the lullaby our dying body clings to as the light fades and shadows of darkness envelop all that we have been, and we dissolve into the sound of love, the sound of surrender, making the easy dissent into the grave of this world—the true passage into Source, into life beyond mystery.

Source is arrival. It is true home, welcome, belonging—no more wandering or wondering.

Source is completion. Neither haste nor regret changes the path to Source. However we navigate the journey, the arrival is the same—into the stillness of the center of all Being.

Warrior Woman

Deep, deep turning, searching,
Screaming loud aloud big searing sound
Through stillness, non-Being to now,
I am warrior woman.

Come from Grandmother of earth,
Of music, of color and design,
Weaving notes and textures with quality of life,
Surrounding the mundane with hope
And pleasure, laughter and beauty.
I know hope and pleasure, laughter and beauty as
They pass through me into my children and beyond,
Singing and dancing, blessing and celebrating life.

Deep, deep turning, burning, being
Alive, alert, awakened to stunning
Pain, hardship, misery, mystery, work,
I am warrior woman.

Come from Grandfathers of work,
Risk, loss, journey into
Tomorrow to find an answer, a direction, a challenge.
Grandfather of business boom bust
Boom boom bust dust hush,
Boom, boom…death.
Job well done.
Father of gentle spirit touching the
Earth, to build and heal,
To teach, to gift, to restore and inspire—
A journey of service, quiet like
Flowers growing, knowing
Telling silently of Truth and Eternity.

Gone early from our circle, his energy fills
And spills forth in my footsteps today.
I am warrior woman.

Born of the Spirit that crashes though
Plans and peaks and valleys
To announce the birthing of wholeness in
The midst of imperfection and strife.
Born of the one who sings
Hallelujahs before the miracle appears,
Allowing all that is to be joined together.
Born of the Spirit who shows the way to those who see,
Who sings to quiet the racing mind and free
Conscioussness into wellbeing and natural intelligence.
I am warrior woman.

I yield to the energy of this Spirit.
It fills me.
I am blessed.
I rise up. I see just now what is, and I am full.
Full of power, full of dreams,
Full of love.
I am spun into a web of
Loving kindness from which
I cannot fall.
I am free from all tension, resentment and self-doubt.
I am warrior woman.

What if Life ...

What if Life gives you a canvass to paint on, and it gives you choices—to be honest or not, to love or not, to try again when you fall short of your own goals, or not. That "or not" part is really important. Who else cares what you paint on your canvass?

What if the answer is: "We all care what you paint." What you paint either inspires us or frightens us. Can you show us the dimensions of what is possible? And can you let us, in return, show you? We could end up being mirrors of life's possibilities, mirrors of Life unfolding. And then?

What if Life demands that we create visions? How do we meet the people who cross our path with stories of possibilities we have never dreamed of? What if we had everything we needed, and then a tornado swept it all away in a moment? Life may give us companions, goals, and challenges, but it also demands that we accept our own defeat. And then?

What if Life isn't safe? What if it gives no guarantees but death? What if we have to make our own meaning out of it? Life is the air, the sun, the days and nights, and the canvass. Tics scurry by looking for something nourishing and tasty. Hurricanes come and go. Fortunes rise and fall. Health is here, then gone. Are we really the authors of meaning? And then?

What if Life simply asks: "And then?" What if it just waits and responds like the good parent, not controlling our choices, only setting the parameters for the consequenses of those choices? What if it holds to its integrity no matter what foibles, tricksters, thieves and liars try to steal the show and rewrite the script? And then?

What if Life knows the games we humans play, and sends warnings when we stray too far from the truth of how Life works? What if some listen, respond, appreciate and defend Life's rules and warning, and others don't?
And then?

Blueberries form on the bushes nearby. A tiny ant crawls across the page. A dragon fly lands on a fence post. And so? Obama rejects or approves the Keystone pipeline. And so? What if we limit our carbon and live, or we don't—and we surely die? And then?

What will we paint?

I Feel Love in My Bones

I feel love in my bones as I remember my young maiden-self full of such courage, clarity and enthusiasm. She tried everything—tap dance, ballet, tumbling, basketball, field hockey, student council, hospital volunteer, Girl Scout. She had her defeats with boyfriends, pimples and body image, yet her inner eagle was learning to soar.

I feel love in my bones when I remember my Mother-self, who knew the fruitfulness of bearing three beautiful sons who have since grown into mature, strong, trustworthy and gentle fathers and husbands. We weathered the tests of unconditional love, forgiveness, and devotion in the midst of diapers, tantrums, football games, alcohol, storming offs and returns—always returns to the heart of our family that could hold the trials and defeats as well as the triumphs. She mothered herself through the turmoil of pain, guilt and ambivalence of leaving a ten year marriage that wasn't right for her life, and headed out to seek a more authentic life.

I feel love in my bones as I now cherish the sage-elder that I have become, who understands gentleness, humility, gratitude and wonder as the most important lessons. Looking back on 70 years of saying "Yes" to life with no regrets, my storybook is full of fascinating people, wondrous faraway places, and satisfying family relationships across the globe (Uganda, Russia, Switzerland, Nicaragua, and Canada). Striving is over. Savoring is the assignment now, and curiosity the ever-present invitation.

I feel love in my bones as I receive moment to moment from Spirit, my most important teacher. I cherish the tests of acceptance that have given me freedom. I watch for the resistance to life in me that signals attachment and leads to suffering. I have let cancer be my teacher about healthier living, and I learned to bend through all the not-knowing controversy surrounding treatment options that led me daily into the mystery of Life and death—into the pondering of how to prepare for my death with an open heart, gratitude and acceptance. This mystery continues to lead me into an ever-surging urgency to drink in more beauty, share more of my own creativity, sing louder, hike higher up the mountain, put more rows in my garden, and never again miss a sunrise, a sunset or a moon rise. I hail each flock of geese that passes overhead on their migration journey, as if they trumpet the way I surely will one day follow.

The Door Opens

I am flying above my life in a dream.
I look down and see a high wall.
I am trapped on one side of the wall
With no way over or around.
I search for a door.
Where is it?
How far do I have to search?
Why is there no door?
I am hopeless, I feel abandoned.
I stand still. I surrender.
A voice says "Let the way open where you stand.
Don't look for it--be it..
What you say and do are your path of learning."
The door appears.
How can this be?
Why didn't I see it before?
Did I have a picture of
how things should be
That kept me from seeing
That when I surrender
My "should"
The door is already there?

The Great Nap

I have been plotting and bargaining with my powerful self to take a Great Nap. That's capital G, capital N. This is not just any ordinary nap. This is a spectacular Nap, a sensual, endless, no-holds-barred Nap. This is the Nap my soul has been craving. This is a Soul Nap. Or is it a soul awakening? Well, soul is in charge. Soul is calling the shots and I am listening.

Oh no—no shots. Stop the shots! Stop the calling of anything! The GN is beginning! But who will take care of Sandra's GNP while I'm a-slumber? Call in the Shadow workers ! I need an alter ego. I need to put zestful Sandra in charge of her GNP so soul can go into nap land. I need to tell her to at least go into the next room where I don't have to listen to her on the phone. No, that's not enough. I need the Nap police to just go and shut her up, so I can figure out how to do this nap thing.

So where does one go to take a Great Nap? What good is all my woman power if I can't even figure this out? What if there is no perfect place? What if the only place is somewhere inside, deep, deep inside, that doesn't listen to the outside anymore? Hum…can one get lost in there if one goes too far? Can the Great Napper lose her way, and never find the pilot of performance again?

I still want to nap, and not the ordinary kind. I want a nap where one dream just merges into the next, with no intermission. I want to be amazed by my own stillness. I want to break my addiction to the phone, the mail, the TV, the e-mail. I want to STOP earning money and paying bills. Oh God, where do I find the conviction to do this?

I can't even stop eating sugar for a day. What do I need to let go of that will put my soul in charge?

I really don't know. I am sad. I make jokes about my Great Nap instead of doing it. I lie to myself as I say "Yes" to one more client wanting my time. The dream shrinks to a half-hour in the hammock, or fighting back the guilt of not answering my e-mail in order to steal an hour with a long-postponed book.

Oh God, my soul wants to turn the world off and stay awake all night reading and reading, pleasuring my hungry being with its deepest desires. I'm praying now. Oh God, I really mean it. Help me. I don't have this power. I don't even know this power. I must not want it bad enough. I settle for pseudo naps—an hour here and there, nothing that plummets me out of this demanding and seemingly powerful life, deep into my soul being. My silent, praying soul is already sitting by the quiet sea at dawn, longing for me to finally care enough to find it. I see now that the Great Nap is already happening, with or without my participation. I don't create it; it is created for me. I have to want it more than all the other trappings of importance.

I am sorry. I am apologizing to my soul for abandoning it for the trappings of responsibility and obligation. I am apologizing for my betrayal of my deepest, most honest desire. Or is my most honest desire to be with my business-as-usual achievement-driven routine, because that is what I am choosing? I let myself glimpse the Great Nap as if it were an unattainable lover who would never choose me, so I am free to fantasize about it.

What would change if I let myself want it enough? I would take enough money out of savings to pay my bills for a year. I would end all my work relationships. Then I would sit still and see what arises. I would build a bay window off my dining room for my plants in the winter. I would paint a mural on my garage wall. I would read my favorite teachers, and maybe Harry Potter, too. I would call up the people I love and tell them. I would play the piano. I would write for the fun of it. I would pray, meditate, and walk every morning. I would be available for fun, adventure, and mystery. Maybe I would live for long stretches in a woods, with just the sounds of nature, until I came to know the ways of that place. My only purpose would be awareness, joy, and peacefulness. Jung built his dream house as a meditation in his later years. Maybe I would build something, but I don't know what.

This is the Great Nap. Imagine no apologies for doing it. Imagine how bold it would be to actually do it. Imagine how my Soul would welcome me to the quiet, relaxed emptiness. Imagine the transformation in my relationship to my driven, performer self. Imagine the grace—that it really would be OK, just fine. Imagine….

Am I Lost?

The voice of being guides me
As I wake to the first light of day,
Noticing the mighty maple branches framing the dawn
Outside my window.
I follow the zippity-do-da trail of the squirrel
Scrambling along a branch
So high above the ground.
I open to a day empty of appointments
And am amused by what I choose to do.
I take an unplanned nap,
Just because the February sun
Is beaming in on my bed
And my big stuffed tiger's soft body is so welcoming.
I give no thought to the grief of death
Until my friend is dying.
Now this voice of being has another focus:
The voice of ending, and
The call of the wild things who know
A time arrives when our being is taken back.
Who decides when?
What happens to being?
Am I lost? Is all lost?
No, I see where I am.
I have lived a long and full life.
I have loved, I have served.
I have been blessed, and I have been a blessing.
There is nothing lost in ending the journey—
Ending the awakening to dawn,
The delight in the squirrel,
The Connections with loved ones—
Now all these will transform,
But are never lost.

I feel the energy of belonging,
Of loving,
Of creating art, music and ritual together.
I feel the presence of others who are part of us,
But absent in body.
I am in the mystery of being right now.
I am clasping hands with all who have gone before,
Oh—a surprise—and all who will come after.
After what?
Hum…after I'm not here in body anymore?
What part does my body have in this great dance of being?
Here comes the grief for my physical body.
Now I am complaining,
Searching for answers.
The voice of being is silenced by
My need to hold on to what I have known,
My need to cry hard,
And feel lost.
I think I'll go lie down with the wild things for a while.

Reunion

The light of guidance is always shining,
Even behind obstacles.
Faith is feeling and following the light
Even when it is hidden.
Light can shine from within too,
As a guide.
I am not the light, but I am in the light.
The light is part of me, yet greater than me.
Sometimes it shines clearly through me,
Then I am quiet, gentle, and kind.
Sometimes I block the light,
Then I lose clarity; I am confused.
I feel insecure. I am afraid.
I feel cold, dark and lonely.
I stop, I breathe, I wait.
I drop down below my mind.
I listen, I pray.
The light always returns,
I know it by its warmth.
It soothes my fear.
The obstacle in me slowly dissolves.
Reunion comes again.

To Savor My Wanderings and Musings

Invitation

Come, blue sky, into my soul.
Come, white heaven cloud, into my reverie.
Come, bird song, into my voice.
Come, soothing sun, into my sadness.
Come, divine love, into my heart.

Bend Down

July, midsummer sun, heat,
Beans, squash, beets,,
Cucumber, green pepper, celery,
Basil, parsley, kale,
Tomatoes, still green but swelling,
All here to touch, to tend.
I bend down to the earth
To eat the sun-rain-soil miracles,
Commune with Life—
To taste it, to savor it,
And bow in thanksgiving
For bounty, for presence,
For meeting God and eating the divine.

God Nectar

Grapes are coming,
Quietly green, clumping
Beneath broad, shading leaves,
Vines climbing through tree branches
Above my garden.
I can already taste your
Biting sweetness, your
Purple glorious gush of God nectar
That I will so joyfully pick, cook, and raise
With friends to toast
Life's wonder and grace.

Mystery

Butterfly, so white against
The colors of the flowers
You so wistfully visit,
Where do you come from?
Where do you go?
Like love—like life itself—
You are so real for a moment,
So here, so beautiful,
And then?

The Altar of Beauty

This morning I go to church in my garden.
The birds are already in their pews.
So, too, are the worms, the butterflies, the ants,
And the slugs.
Together we worship
At the altar of beauty,
The altar of life giving life to life,
While the winged choir sings hallelujah.

Parade

Earth opens her banquet before me,
A parade of creation unfolding,
With birds, flowers, and sky all serenading in harmony.
I am drinking in God.
I listen to the music,
I smell the earth blooming,
I open to take in more,
As I sit watching the celebration.
Oh! Surprise!
Suddenly I jump into the parade with
My flag and my horn.
I cheer for life, for God, for the parade,
For the sheer joy of Being!

Open Heart

Long ago mighty maple,
Now transformed by carver's knife
Into a saint here in my backyard,
Welcome Buddha, open heart Buddha,
Arms stretched in jubilation,
With tender hands, neither grasping nor averting,
Open-palmed, open, open,
Spirit a-twinkle,
Head tilted just so
To greet, to meet
Any pilgrim on the path,
Any unsuspecting visitor who thought
They came for another reason,
But then they meet you.

God is in My Garden

God is in my garden,
Red and yellow, orange and magenta bobbing miracles,
Each a note in the serenade of the catbird
Singing to Spirit
From the branch above.
Church bells chime,
Sun beams touch leaf,
Vegetables swell on their vine,
Ants crawl,
Bees buzz,
Birds swoop,
And I am divine
Here in my garden.

If Mother Nature is Family

How would our lives be different if Mother Nature really is our mother? She would be someone we'd think about in a family way—like "How are you doing today? Any troubles? Any need for support? Any joys or concerns?" Then we'd have to really listen, like really care and really make ourselves available if Mother Nature is having a bad day, or dealing with an unfortunate assault on her rights to be free or be treated with dignity.

We'd have to go to bat for Her—be Her voice—so she wouldn't have to communicate as a hurricane, a wildfire, or a tornado. We'd have to make sure She is comfortable and secure so She wouldn't have to announce her complaints with a flood or a drought.

We'd get to have holidays with Her, planning how to celebrate Her seasons and the shifts in Her supply and demand system of production. That would mean doing without certain foods and comforts in lean seasons, and sharing abundance in prolific seasons. We'd be following Her lead, paying attention to Her changing needs. We would be at Her beck and call.

We would be willing to take feedback when She is upset or frustrated, like when we aren't doing a good enough job. We'd have to take the lead in removing some of the barriers to Her freedom to thrive, like stopping mountain top removal and outlawing oil pipelines that leak.

We would sing lullabies in the late evening to all Her creatures who inhabit the land we share. We'd swing in a hammock after dark and listen to the symphony of peepers singing back to us. We'd fill the bird feeder whenever it is empty to be sure no one goes hungry on our watch. We'd go to meetings about regulating what gets released into the air, and we'd protest the mining of oil that, if burned, would choke our atmosphere with carbon.

At bedtime, Mother Nature would snuggle in with us to read a story about Her many cycles of birth and death and rebirth. She would tell us of magnificent ancient beasts roaming the earth, or tiny insects in the soil that transform dirt into food. We would feel very loved. We would go to sleep knowing we are in good hands.

She's willing.

Spring's Arising

May, oh say,
I sing today,
Saying hello to tree and sky,
Not even knowing the reason why
They have bloomed into being
With a job to do
Drinking in rain, turning sunlight to food
For root and trunk and flower divine,
For bird to nest and insect to dine.

Oh the joy of being part of a tree,
A virtual neighborhood for all to see!
Giving shade and shelter to bee and dove,
To microbes below and squirrels above.
Oh leaf, oh tree, I see I see
Spring arising through you
And arising through me.

Springing through bud and bee, passing life to each other,
Sharing pollen and nectar, what could be kinder?
Spring-swing-sway oh say
Can you see, too, the bold cardinal and yakking blue jay?
Sporting their fancy coats to charm the dames,
While rivaling the sunrise's brilliant flames
As they greet God and the dawn with merry delight,
Before grabbing a worm, and then taking flight.

Dark Spark

Oh seed, you lady-in-waiting,
What are you waiting for?
Water wakes you up,
And you swell and transform.
Oh, a new shoot cracks open the pod
And heads for the sun.
Where are you going?.
Are you an idea? A song? A poem?
Did I think you up, or
Stumble upon you?
Should I be quiet,
Or plan for a resurrection?
Such an adventure, you.
Should I go take a nap,
Or clear a garden?
Or send out invitations?
What makes you grow?
Dark spark of creation,
You hold me in suspense
Until you are ready.
Will I dare to follow?

Sing a Song of Summer

Sing a song of summer
The squash is taking over,
Growing vines mount beans and flowers
Twisting forth with frequent showers.
I tend, I weed, I plant again.
I pick. I munch, I sing a hymn
To birds, to worms, to taste, to color
Abundance fills tummy, cupboard and more
Spills out to critter and neighbor
Joined in the feast for all to savor.

Come Silence

Come silence fill me now.
Nothing to do.
Nothing to be.
Nothing to say.
Nothing to see.
Nothing to feel.
Empty.
Spacious.
Timeless.

No words.
No sounds.
No thoughts.
Quiet now.
Endless.
I bow.
I smile.
I wait.
I am Life appearing,
Disappearing,
Playing peek-a-boo
Among the stars
While the universe laughs.

Welcome Bodhi

Looking out, what do you see?
Blurry figures, then tastes, touch and sound.
You feel the embrace that beckons you into being,
And oh, the smell of mother!
Oh, the vital feeling of sucking and filling—
You are already an expert at life's first assignment.
Resting on daddy's shoulder, snuggling to mother's breast,
You are sensing your safety,
Building your trust one episode of alarm at a time.

Other voices, other touch—
A circle of hands holds you strong,
Welcomes you to the two clans now
Made one by your arrival.
You touch our deepest memory of beginnings.
You bring us close to God.
You stir our hope for a better world.
You offer us total vulnerability,
Which awakens our deepest caring.

You—so tiny—embody the miracle of journey
From seed to fruit.
You bring generations, time, and history to light,
So hidden in the shadows of our busy lives.
You slow us down to notice the moment—
The eye lash, the fingernail white with the
Tightness of your tiny grip.
You show off the detail of ear
Wrinkle, glance, grip, stretch,
Yawn—all so familiar, yet

Unremarkable until you do it.
You call forth giggles, coos, and babbles from us.
You lead us into baby land
Where our own adulthood dissolves into
Play, cuddle, and awe.
Welcome, Bodhi.

Love, Grandma Sandra

I Know I Am Home

I know I am home when I look into my cat's staring eyes. He is always home. He is always waiting for me to sit down so he can climb into my lap and push up between me and the newspaper until all I can see is him. He places his two front paws in the center of my chest and settles down there. Max is doing his "heart to heart;" he knows he has a job to do. He is the only one in my life who seeks out my beating heart so deliberately. He brings me home.

I know I am home when I bend down to weed my garden. These are my weeds. No one else will see them or care that they are growing bigger every day. Only I know the plants between them that need protecting. Only I have the gardener's picture of how the garden will look when the favored plants have reached maturity. I know I am home when I see them blossoming into fullness and lending their voices to the symphony of beauty that sings to me of home.

I know I am home when I reach in the mailbox and find a love letter from a far-away friend. I feel the presence of a heart beating across the invisible bridge built with care and memory. We commune there on my front porch as I open the envelope. We slowly begin to dance in an embrace as I unfold the letter. Soon the laughter of playfulness or the tears if recognition—shared pain—transform the porch into a temple with gently tingling bells of ancient origin. I hold a story in my hands, and a loved one in my heart—my true home.

I know I am home when I climb into bed, turn out the light, and stare at the moon peeking through the towering branches of the sugar maple outside

my window. I follow the seasons through the
lifecycle of this tree, so full with leaves now that the
moon is barely visible. In winter, the moon is
Queen of the Sky, and the tree's bare skeleton is her adoring
courtesan. In spring, she will burst forth with new life,
greeting me at dawn with shouts of, "Come out and play!"
She is the guardian of my home, and we are family.

I am home when the house is quiet and my eyes come
to rest on the painting above the mantle in the living
room that my mother painted after she visited Nepal.
She called it "Kathmandu." It is her interpretation of the
energy of the Himalayas, bright blue, white and green
clouds surging above and around a tiny splash of orange.
It is quietly magnificent, carrying ancestral energy.

I am home when my eyes gaze around the empty living
room—place of so many gatherings—the walls vibrating
with plans, dreams, hopes and celebrations. I am there
amidst the throng of chatter, drum, song and story—in
the enchantment of so many hearts beating together. I
am home in this humming, clamoring, bursting forth of
laughter, tears, and determination that is community.

I am home when I pause on my morning walk through
the forest, turn toward the dawn breaking on the
horizon, and pray silently to the giver of life, daily
renewing my offering to love, to forgive, to be peace, to
never give up, and to always give thanks for my life.

To Be Surprised by Wit, Humor, and Life Laughing at Itself

Why Not Fly?

If I could but a poem be,
I'd fly myself to the top of a tree.
From there I'd scan horizons grand
And take flight for an enchanted land.

I'd fly up the river to tumbling falls,
And perch where the sound my ear enthralls.
Wet from rising mist, I'd ponder
In what other direction I want to wander.

Off I'd fly to forest thick,
And land on a blooming bush I'd pick.
And watch honeybees going to and fro,
While spying on fawn and doe below.

Oh, the miracle of life, of color galore!
Where else shall I launch and further explore?
Up I fly to the mountain with rocky crag,
Where I watch darting swallows in a game of tag.

Sun setting now, it's time to head home,
To settle back down and cease to roam.
What fun to be a poem with elegant flair,
While never having to leave my chair.

Max

Max was my cat for 15 years.
He followed me everywhere I went in the house.
He waited for me on my computer keyboard,
Then he climbed into my lap when I sat down.
I loved staring into his unblinking eyes.
He always stared right back.
I was looking at God.

I was looking at God
He always stared right back.
I loved staring into his unblinking eyes.
Then he climbed into my lap when I sat down.
He waited for me on my computer keyboard,
He followed me everywhere I went in the house.
Max was my cat for 15 years.

Lorraine

I'm in the third grade, and every time we have recess I stare at Lorraine on the playground. She has long, blonde, curly hair and bright blue eyes. She has an ease to her moving that I admire, maybe even envy. She is certainly popular. No question. Ah, but what about me? Lots of questions. Am I pretty? I really don't know. Is there anything about me that other kids would envy the way I envy Lorraine? How do you get to be popular?

I ponder this question so relentlessly, it seems like the only important question. Somehow math problems and music lessons come and go like the days of the week, but that one question is as big as is there a God. Now God can wait. I know I don't have to answer that question soon—it could take a lifetime. But this one about how to be popular, well it can't wait. Actually, I should already know. But I don't. It's probably already too late, like I missed the boat, or the lucky charms were all passed out by God and He ran out before He got to me.

So I just watch Lorraine. I watch how she talks to people. I watch how she sits on her chair. I watch how she carries her books. I watch her comb her gorgeous hair in the bathroom. Every day I eagerly look for her first thing to study what she is wearing and who she is talking to. Sometimes, I even dare to stand near her and even—even—risk saying something to see if she will look at me and respond, or if she will act like she doesn't hear me and turn away to talk to the other popular girls. My heart rides on her response like a twig on the surf, easily lifted and let down with no volition of its own. I study the freckles on her face. I think you have to have blonde hair to have freckles. They're so cute. They remind me of Bambi and his spots. Everyone loves Bambi too—he's cute, too, and little, and adorable. Me, I'm chubby and awkward. I'm even shy, so unsure of what others think of me. I don't know what to think of myself. I just know I never have the attention that Lorraine and Bambi have.

Maybe if I thought more about the God question God would help me. But I just can't get there from where I am, riveted on Lorraine's every move. Sometimes I get so involved in climbing the jungle gym I forget about all these big questions for a moment or two. I swing upside down, feeling the air, the blood rushing to my head, the strength in my legs, and the thrill of daring to let my hands fall free. But then I spot her over there on the swings—so graceful and sweet. I suddenly realize how different I am from Lorraine, and the disappointment knocks all the fun out of my swing. I come back to my senses, and back to that big haunting question. Somehow God and Lorraine have the answer, and the unanswered question is "Who am I?"

Even in Sunday school, when Mr. Sunberg tells us that Jesus loves us, I wonder if Jesus loves Lorraine more than me because she's pretty, and graceful, and popular, and I don't know who I am. I just know I'm not any of those things. I wonder if Jesus was popular. Seems people followed him and believed him, but he died on a cross so that doesn't seem very popular. But he still got to be God's son anyway. Could that mean there is hope for me? Maybe I should have figured out that God thing. It may be my only ticket.

I wonder if Lorraine believes in God. Did God make her popular? If he made her popular, how come he didn't make Jesus popular? Oh God, how can there be any help for me? Jesus even had long hair like Lorraine. Maybe I should grow my hair long too. But my hair is thin, and it isn't curly. It gets all crooked and whacky when I sleep on it. I don't think Lorraine ever has to worry about her hair. It just curls and tumbles behind her sparkling blue eyes effortlessly—like her popularity. I bet she never even thinks about her hair.. She must be God's favorite.

Maybe I should have prayed more. What would I pray? "Oh God, could you make my hair curly?" Or is it the blonde part that makes you popular? Oh dear, I don't even know how to pray right. It's hopeless! I'm doomed to watch Lorraine on the swings, stuck up here on the jungle gym with my underwear showing—which I know isn't cool, but I haven't figured out what to do about that either. What does Lorraine do about that? Hum… I've never seen her underwear show. I've never seen her on the jungle gym. I guess popular girls don't climb and hang upside down. So why am I up here staring down at her? How did I get here? Who am I? Does God know I'm stuck up here without a clue?

God didn't save Jesus when he was stuck up on the cross, so I doubt if He'll be much help to me now. Maybe if I'd stayed with the God question I wouldn't be up here with my underwear showing and my hair straight, staring at Lorraine on the swing. I guess some girls are just meant to hang on a cross and others get away scot free.

My Grandmother is a Bag Lady

In the voice of my six year old grandson Bodhi

My grandmother is kinda strange. She's always saving things everybody else thinks is trash. She has a closet full of boxes—all sizes—ready to wrap something in that she bought at a tag sale. You never get anything new from my grandmother, 'cause she doesn't go to stores to buy presents. She even saves old bottles and cans and newspapers and cardboard boxes to give to the recycle man.

I ask her why she saves everything. At the time she is refolding wrapping paper at a birthday party. Why doesn't she just throw it away like everyone else? She tells me the paper is beautiful. She doesn't want to throw away anything that can be used again if it is beautiful.

I think the paper is pretty too, but then why doesn't anyone else think so? She also tells me that things you buy—like pretty paper—cost money. The more money you spend, the more you have to earn, and that means going to work. She tells me she wants to need as little money as possible so she will have more time in her life to walk in the woods and read and play the piano instead of having to earn money. I like to do those things too. I'm glad she likes to do them with me. Maybe I'll save pretty paper, too, when I'm grown up, so I can play more.

She also tells me that a Native American (I'm not sure what that is) once taught her that it is important to walk lightly on the earth. I ask her does that mean to tip toe? She says no, it means only taking what you really need, and leaving the rest for someone else. ("The rest of what?" I think, but I don't ask 'cause I want her to think I understand what she is saying.) I can tell it's something really important to her. She says it's about living simply, not trying to be the best or have the most, but living close to the earth.

"What does living simply mean, grandma?" I ask. She tells me everything comes from the earth. Everything we use is made from something that can just be picked up or dug up in its natural form and then used to make something we buy. Sometimes it's food and we just pick it and eat it. "Like apples?" "Yes, and strawberries," she adds. "Sometimes it's a mineral like oil or iron ore and we have to do work to change it into something like gas or aluminum so we can use it. The more money we have to spend to change it, the more valuable—or costly—it becomes," she continues. She goes on talking about those big questions about money, time and work, and what they have to do with being happy. Somehow they're all related, and the simpler the better.

She tells me that a lot of people waste gas and aluminum because they don't think about where those things come from and what it costs to make them. All of a sudden, I can feel my grandmother getting very sad and very serious. "There's a lot more to it when it comes to gas for our cars, because we even have to get the oil that makes the gas from countries far away, and sometimes we don't get along with those countries so we even go to war and kill people so we can get that oil," she presses on. I'm hoping she will change the subject and cheer up, but it gets worse. "Then people still waste the gas driving big cars." I'm afraid she's going to get very upset. I wonder if my Daddy drives a big car. I'm a little worried that grandma will find out and be mad at him. "So is this right, grandma," I venture, " that living simply means not needing big cars so we use less gas so people don't need something that costs so much, even somebody's life sometimes?" "That's it, dear."

Now I'm starting to understand a little about living simply and a lot about my grandmother. I ask her about the cans and bottles. She keeps them in a bin on her front porch and puts them out on her curb once a week where they are picked up and sent back to the people who put things in them so those people don't have to make more bottles or cans. It's kind of like a big circle of some kind. I can tell that circle makes my grandmother happy. She smiles when she talks about it.

"But grandma, what's the point of that circle if you can just go to the store and get more cans and bottles anyway?" I'm not prepared for what comes next. It's like a science lesson. My grandmother is very smart, and she thinks about how everything is connected. She tells me glass is made from sand, and there's lots of it around, and its cheap. Everything liquid used to come in bottles before they made milk cartons and aluminum cans. The paper used to make milk cartons comes from trees. People chop down real living trees just to get paper—a whole tree!—when they could just use cheap sand. Grandmother loves the trees, and besides, she says the trees make oxygen that we need to breathe, and they make a home for thousands (how does she know all this?) of other wild creatures in forests. She says some trees make medicine, too. We should never cut down a tree unless it is absolutely necessary. I like trees too. I like to climb them. I don't want to hurt trees. Why would anyone chop down a tree if they could use sand instead?

Then she tells me if I put a bottle in the ground and leave it for a year, it will still be there when I dig it up. So it takes up space in a place called a land fill. She tells me so many people throw so many bottles and cans away that we are running out of places to put them. Since bottles can be used again if we put them out on the curb on recycle day, why put them in the earth where they become a problem? I agree with her.

Then she starts explaining more about soda and beer cans. Things get really complicated—really over my head—but I listen as best I can because I can tell how important all this is to her, and no one has ever explained this to me before about living lightly on the earth. But I can feel that there is something pretty heavy about this living lightly thing, like it's a fight of some kind and people take sides. I haven't ever even thought about actually living *on* the earth, as if that is an important thing to think about. The earth is like a person to my grandmother—like a neighbor you want to be sure to get along with because you might need help or be needed to help sometime. I like my neighbors the McCoys, because they let me swing on their swings and they have flowers and a dog I can play with. The neighbors on the other side aren't friendly. They don't say hello and all the kids know not to go in their yard or you get yelled at. We never go to their door on Halloween. I guess they don't' care about being neighbors.

Well my grandmother sure does care about being a good neighbor. But she's talking about the earth, not the people next door. The earth is a pretty big neighborhood. I can see how much she likes being in that neighborhood. Oops, I forgot to listen for a minute, and she is going on about the soda cans. She's talking about nuclear power and electricity. I know what electricity is—something in the switch that makes a light go on, but I don't know where it comes from or what on earth it has to do with soda cans. I listen, because I can tell it's very important to grandmother and has something to do with being good neighbors, and I know what that feels like.

She says cans start out being iron ore you can dig up right out of the earth. But to turn that into aluminum takes five times as much electricity as to make a bottle from sand. It takes a lot of heat to melt the ore and turn it into aluminum. You have to make aluminum; you can't just dig it up. So it costs a lot of money to make it because they have to buy the electricity to heat it. Here's where I get a little lost. The more cans you need, the more electricity you need, and the electricity is very expensive. Well, some of it isn't if it comes from some kind of dam across a big river, 'cause its what she calls a natural force. Nobody made the water or the river, they just built a dam in order to make electricity as the water runs through it. Sounds simple.

But more and more electricity is needed when people need more things like cans and cars made of aluminum. So they found a way to make electricity using something called uranium. Problem is, this uranium, which you can dig up, has to be turned into something else—I think she said plutonium—before they can get it to make electricity. When they change it to plutonium, something really dangerous happens. Grandmother's voice gets deeper when she is telling me this part. I can tell she is angry. It feels like the bad neighbor thing. Plutonium hurts people. It makes them sick if they get near it. If it leaks out of the place they make the electricity, it can even kill a lot of people.

So my grandmother says when we throw away things made with aluminum its like putting in an order for more electricity, and that means asking for more plutonium to be made. When we save our cans and reuse them, we don't need more plutonium. I don't want people to die or get sick because of my soda can.

And then she goes back to the whole space thing. The people in New York City have a lot of garbage, and they live on an island so they can't bury it. So they put it on great big boats and take it out and dump it into the sea. Some of it makes the fish sick, and some of it washes up on beaches where kids are swimming. I like to go to the ocean and play in the waves. I don't want to step on someone's garbage there. Yuck!

I see grandmother stuffing newspaper into a garbage bag and putting it into her car. What is she going to do with it? "Why can't you throw that in the trash, grandma?" I'm prepared to hear another story about being neighbors and walking lightly, but I don't expect to hear about someone living in the tippy top of a giant old tree in order to save it from being chopped down. All grandmother's stories are about big things—big dams, big piles of garbage, and big problems like plutonium. Me, I'm just living here in my own house, drinking my soda and watching Daddy read the paper. How does my grandmother know so much? How come every question I ask goes back to the same story about how we live on the earth? Why doesn't' anyone else talk about this on TV or at school? My grandmother seems weird, but her stories make sense. I get ready to hear about the lady in the tree and the bulldozer down below. Somehow this is all related to the garbage bags in her car.

To Pray through My Pen, from Soul to Source

God of This Crystal-Clear Morning

Oh God of this crystal-clear morning,
I see you in the dew drops
Sparkling like tiaras on every blade of grass,
Every leaf tip, every petal.
I am surrounded by your touch, your presence.
I smell the essence of fresh.
I feel a breeze caressing my face.
The warm rays of sun crossing vast space reach
Through my jacket and warm my soul.
I wait—still, and open.
You greet me in crow's caw
From a-top my nearby hemlock.
Good morning crow.
Good morning life.
Good morning God.

Transition

Flowers are fading,
Shadows lengthen,
Nights grow colder.
Peaches still ripening, raspberries too.
Early fall, transition.
Everything still green, but soon to turn.
We know it, yet we look at the thermometer
Hoping it will rise as the day progresses-
And it does, for just a while longer.
Sky, so brilliant blue—not the soft summer blue–
Is crisp like the air as days shorten.
Pick the last tomatoes today, and cucumbers.
The kale, broccoli, and parsley will last a while longer.
Goodbye, and thank-you, garden-soil-worm-microbes.
Thank-you.

Praise

Praise Great Spirit present in all living beings, honoring the holiness of plants, animals, water, air and soil.

Praise communities where people are living on the earth in acceptance and reverence for the way they found it.

Praise the flowing of water, always toward the sea.

Praise journeying by kayak, with paddle dipping into fog-shrouded, early dawn-still lake.

Praise the calling of the loon—just out of sight— bringing the presence of Spirit to the moment.

Praise the dawn bird song, and red cardinals visiting the bird feeder outside my window.

Praise rays of light mottling the forest floor—sun kissing the earth.

Praise new shoots of green, poking up through the soil to feed soul as well as body.

Praise grandchildren jumping, jibbering and jiving with devices made of tomorrow.

Praise community and family, weaving the web of life with each other—the web coming alive and visible through smiles, tears, plans and changes.

Praise good books teaching us about ourselves, and about love, time, worthiness and miracles.

Praise works of art calling forth holiness, and the silent chanting of nature.

Praise the heavens with galaxies stretching beyong our knowing.

Praise the crop circles and UFOs hinting of other worlds
and beings who reach across the void to connect.

Praise the ancients, drawing forth the labyrinth
from the silent lay lines of earth so we would have
a path to follow to the center of creation.

Praise home—tending us with food for body, mind and heart,
making a safe harbor for us to return to— a place of soul—
holding us safely through the dark night, and blessing us
on our way with loving, lessons, leavings and return.

King David's 23rd Psalm to the Great Mother

The hand of the Great Mother rocks the cradle of my soul,
I shall not want.
She shows me how to lie down in green pastures.
She leads me beside the still waters.
She restores my soul.
Yea, though I walk through the valley of the shadow of death,
I will not fear,
For She is with me.
Her song and her touch, they comfort me.
She blesses my whole being with her kiss.
She prepares a table before me in the presence of my limitations.
My cup overflows.
Surely, goodness and mercy shall surround
And fill me all the days of my life,
And I will dwell in the heart of the Mother forever.

My Birthday Prayer

Oh Great Spirit within all of Life, who gifts us with our being,
I pray in gratitude for:

Being loved and cherished by my family and friends.

Being surrounded by beauty in my garden,
my home, and my community.

Having time to write my story and share it with others.

Swinging gently in the hammock with leisure and solitude.

Connecting with dear friends over years
and years of sharing life's journey.

Discovering poetry that makes my soul sing.

Hearing good news about how one person cared for another.

Feeling the textures of silk, wool, llama fur, snake
skin, and my pet Max's soft fur against my cheek.

Tasting the special moment when
chocolate melts on my tongue.

Hearing a grandson whisper "I love you Grandma"
after the story is done and the light is turned off.

Witnessing the green sprouts of Spring pushing
through the snow, announcing the change that is yet
to come—no, already here—along with sap rising
and buds swelling. How do they know it's time?

Being surrounded by a wisdom greater than my own,
announcing itself in such obvious, tangible ways.

Listening to my body as it continually heals,
repairs, anticipates, and communicates its needs
in ways I can hear, understand and tend.

Watching my three sons become loving, attentive, engaged
fathers, and my grandchildren thriving under their guidance.

Searching, always open and waiting for the next
surprise of life's mystery unfolding and unending.

I pray that we might all be blessed with:

Truly caring for every soul.
Respecting and cherishing life in all its forms.

Never taking more than we need in order to
be sure there is enough to go around.

Giving equal opportunity to all children to engage
with life's gifts, blessings and opportunities.

Never littering out of respect for Nature and one another.

Singing for the joy of praising and dancing,
for the joy of feeling oneness,

Feeling safe, loved, whole, creative and valued for our Being.

Holding life as sacred, and providing the basic
essentials to a life of dignity for every person.

Working together to preserve the Earth's
environment for future generations to enjoy
and be nurtured by as we have been.

Inspiring a global movement to replace
killing with healing between people.

Celebrating and honoring the beauty and
uniqueness of all the world's people.

Walking this earth path humbly as guests, admitting our
short-comings and being grateful for how we are loved,
forgiven, accepted and provided for in our imperfections.

Amen... Aho... And so might it be.

Clearing the Deck

Quiet…Still…Alone…Secluded,
Conscious of choice,
I surrender,
Allowing life to unfold.
Halt to plans, connections, responsibilities,
Free fall…flight…wings….drift…soar,
Surprise…
"I am happy with you," the Grandmother blesses me.
"You are never alone. You dance in my heart.
Someday the path ahead will open out and dissolve
Into the Sea of Existence
Where there is only memory, pure awareness,
No ego, no past-present-future,
Just is-ness, released from earth's hold.
So relish life, each plant, flower, seed, creature,
Spring rain,
Each gift from a friend,
Each meal a gift from earth and sun,
Each song an anthem of existence.
Let the melodies play up your spine.
Feel your body alive, happy, open.
Let worries be washed clean by the tide.
Utter thanks for the beauty of it all.
Open."

Grandchild A-Borning

Sammy Boston 3/29/13

Spark, division, energy, sensation,
Brain, spine, finger, toe,
Heart, heartbeat fast, fast, fast,
Muscle electricity contract, relax, expand,
Curl up in out,
Move leg, arm, hand,
Swim, turn, open,
Fluid inside,
Fluid outside,
Blood vessels contract, expand,
Nativity coming, coming, growing fast—
Yet slow.
Eyes, ears, hair, nails,
Knees, ankles, bone,
Growing everywhere.
Cells feeding, releasing mother food
Coming, leaving
Belly swelling, swelling, swelling,
Breasts filling, filling, tight, hard, firm.
Inner universe full of heart beat
Sound and muted voices.
Nativity coming,
Swelling, pending,
Mother no longer bend,ing, waiting
Waiting full up, coming,
Roaring throat, wild sound—
Now!

Nativity opening
Splitting, spilling, splashing open,
Open, come forth
Babe now into arms.
Eyes, tears, light,
Wrap tight,
Tender looking,
Holding close,
Quiet now.
Grandchild snuggled in.

Be the Way

Let the way open where you stand.
Don't look for it—become it.
Open and watch.
What you say and do are the way—
Your path of learning.
The way is defining your truth, though
You may not know it yet.
You will find others who want to walk with you,
Or you may join their path when you find synchronicity.
Veer away when change comes.
Let it have its way and you will change.
Your truth will change.
Don't be afraid to let go and not know what will arise.
There is a guide within the confusion.
It's light shines, even behind obstacles
That hide what is yet to be understood or transformed.
The light is always shinning.
Sometimes you make choices that block the light,
Not knowing you are being the obstacle.
When the light is hidden,
It is cold, dark, and lonely.
You are afraid.
Stop, breathe, wait.
Drop down, listen.
In your stillness the light permeates your being
And the obstacle dissolves.
You and the light become one.
You are warm again.
The way is open.

Winter Solstice

Darker now, darker.
Cold.
Days shorter.
The mystery of night expands.
Cold causes us to cuddle closer,
Crystal frost crunches under foot,
Paints miracles on windows.
Snowflakes flutter on eyelashes.
Fire burns, warms the home.
Dreams deepen in the long dark.
Stars shine brighter.
Barren tree skeletons against the winter sky
Show graceful limbs,
Hidden by summer's canopy.
Everything is quieter now.

Goddess gifts us with night,
Cloak of darkness,
Starkness,
Releases producers to rest,
To trust, in letting go,
That the deep wisdom of earth
Will know just when to re-emerge and grow
Without our even asking
Or telling.
It just will.

Rest in this great intelligence for now.
Stop.
Wait.
Empty.
Deep well.

Bottom.
Stillness.
Still within.
Winter.
Winter stillness.
Winter solstice.

Then Goddess throws the switch.
The planet responds,
Turning ever so slightly
Back towards the light.
No hurry.
All is in balance.
Cold, barren earth.
No stirring.
No feeding.
Only time moves
As oh, so slightly
The earth tips towards the sun.
Ancient rhythm,
Heart beat far below,
Within
Resonates with stars,
Planets, Galaxies,
Tipping ever so slightly
Towards the light.
Dark, dark,
Towards the light.
Mystery deep within
Keeps sap in roots
Until there is enough light
For leaves to feed.
Then it will rise again
Answering the call.

But for now, rest.
Now, peace within
And without.
Stars dance to the nocturne of night.
Goddess watches over her nesting creatures.
Fire crackles.
Frost sparkles.
Dream deepens.
Root is patient.
Soul is still.
Solstice.

To Redeem a Loss or Hurt and to Search for Redemption

Hear the Earth Crying

Hear the earth crying—
Don't we know?
Don't we care?
The plankton and the trees breathe this planet alive.
We can't live without them, yet we cut down
The trees to use for other things.
We let the ice caps melt, acidifying the oceans
Until the plankton can't survive.
We don't see the trees being cut deep in the Amazon forest.
We don't see the ice caps melting, crashing into the sea.
Oh humans, we just don't see!
Like a marriage that is going bad,
But no one is asking why.
Like a car with a knocking sound in the engine,
But no one is looking under the hood.
Like a young person on drugs, making their bargain
With the devil for a few days of high, but…
Can we feel the mounting heat?
Hear that crashing sound?
See those glazed over eyes?
The earth is crying.
Listen.
Hear.
She is us.

What is Being Taken?

Descent, moment to moment,
I watch, I feel, I shutter.
Words wander through my awareness.
Something precious and profound
Is being taken.

What is being taken?
Time, dream, youth, aspiration, safety, the future?
The earth is screaming, reeling out of balance,
Yet we refuse to see.
The chance for resilience and renewal
Is slipping silently away.

What is being taken?
Pride, specialness, stunning human invention,
Replaced with failure, forlorn, regret?
Who will name the terrible loss and
Mourn the crashing hopes
As buildings crumble and fields fall fallow?
Who will remember what was lost?

What is being taken?
Any chance that we will survive these planetary changes
With soul and sanity intact?
Oh my God— whatever holds it all—
Forgive us for what we have not done
To protect this gift of life for future generations.

What is being taken?
A sense of continuity,
Of the goodness of the world as a place to live?
Of security in food, water, weather, old age?
Of community holding together?

May we find traces of that connection we once shared
In the simpler forms of living our survival must take.

What is being taken?
The freedom to be asleep?
To ignore the consequences of what we have done
With our hunt for energy, convenience, comfort, and
Protection from the vulnerability of life itself?
May we learn to cherish Nature's cycles
Of renewal and rebirth
As we seek our own.

What is being taken?
A sense of all the time in the world to do whatever—
Relax, and let go?
No! Now there is urgency—
Wake up! Wake up!
Don't go back to sleep!
Slow down, scale down, drop down
Into your deepest knowing.
Survival of our great-grandchildren depends on
Every choice we make NOW about how we live,
And what degree of comfort and Con-
venience we claim for ourselves
At their expense.

What is being taken?
Any sense of separation from Nature,
Any sense that we humans get to say what is true?
Nature is commanding us to return to
The consciousness of One World,
One life force, one survival,
One hope,
NOW.

And what, pray tell, is being given?
It's our turn.

Four Millimeters

How big is the cancer?
Four what?
What is a millimeter?
Never seen one.
Milli—doesn't that mean 1000?
1000 what?
Units of measure?
Units of flesh? No, tumor.
Units of time I have left?
Units of waiting for the next shoe to fall?
What's next?
Next to me in my breast...
Is it really me? Part of me?
Not a foreign invader rampaging through
The countryside of my breast?
It's next to the duct,
The milk duct that flowed white and nutritious
So long ago, fallow now.
Surprise visitor, this four millimeter lump, announcing itself
On my mammogram,
On my pathology report,
On my answering machine—"call your surgeon."
"DCIS, no problem, eminently treatable,"
He said the first time.
Oops, no, micro-invasion now—it's outside the duct.
It climbed the wall, burst the seam
When I wasn't looking,.
Diagnosis changes now: in-fil-tra-ting car-cin-o-ma
Lilting, isn't it, almost musical in four-part time...
Infiltrating carcinoma, basanova, Barcelona,
Carcinoma, melanoma, Red Sedona...
The music carries me

Into a new chapter in my life
Ringing with the vowel "ah."
Ah, introduction to seven syllable words, machines, and
People in white coats with little time to
linger beyond fact for person.
I become a statistic: three in ten die.
Are these good odds? Bad odds?
How odd to find myself in this story.
How odd to wonder on which side of the divide I will fall,
Or what garden I will grow as I move among the rows
Of tests and questions.

Mystery of Belonging

Yet again
We come to the edge of understanding,
You and me together, yet apart,
Hoping, yet resisting.
You peer forward—is it safe?
Pull back—not sure.
Too far back?
Reach across?
Will I be there?
Where is the balance of belonging?
What do your tears say?
"I'll be OK." No words.
A mystery, you.
Come into my arms,
Just come.
And you did.
And we are
Together,
A mystery,
Belonging.

Hearts See

Hearts see past what is.
Hearts hope—like crocuses in early spring—
For the warmth of being welcomed and safe.
Some—blooming too early—get stepped on and crushed.
Others survive the step, somehow crumpled
But still determined to bloom.
Those fortunate ones bloom enough times
To remind us all to hope.
And so our hearts see.

If only I had such a heart
And I, like it, could withstand the crunch,
I would feel beneath the fray of
Frazzled dreams and frantic efforts
My bruised heart blooming forth.
I would see her, complete in her being,
Bumbling forth, with
Vulnerability, and laughter,
Giving all of herself to work and play,
To adventure and solitude,
Fearless in the presence of enemies,
Gentle in the presence of loved ones,
Fearless and gentle with herself,
And wrapped in my arms.

The Altar of Kindness

She is gone.
I am drowning in grief.
I am not yet willing to let her go.
I hold on. I wail.
I will not let my anger melt. I need it to survive.
I am hurt. I am afraid.
Am I unlovable? A failure?
What do I not understand about love?
Can this pain ever find its way to forgiveness?
Guide within, help me find my way.
Back to trust in my own goodness,
And hers?
The heart surely knows how, but I'm not ready.
I can't? I won't?
How long will I suffer?
I hear a voice within saying "Now."
I'm so tired. I am still afraid.
I know what to do. I pretend I don't know.
Trust beckons again. Let go.
I surrender my rage on the altar of kindness.

Still I Sing

You haunt me even as I hate you
For not turning towards me with a desire
To match my own.
Angry, I wait again
To be desired, loved, and cherished.
Wait again to sing of love to another.
Longing colors my day gray.
Night's darkness a cloak wrapped around my loneliness.
Alone, my song—somber and sad—
Does not evoke a song sung in return.
Still I sing.

Honey Pot

"Oh bother," said Pooh.
"Time for a little something."
Honey pot is empty.
Have to go visit Rabbit.
I knock.
There's a voice.
What? No one there?
Who said "There's no one there?"
Honey pots hide behind fears
Of being eaten up.

Wait a Minute

Sparkling with joy-full delight you are,
New friend, so faithful, awake, drumming the
Heartbeat of the Mother,
Loving, strong and constant…
Wait a moment,
Please—just a moment
For a tender touch
From a new friend
Who just loves to sit by you,
Look at you, and
Be still with you.
"OK," you say, "Just for a moment."
Then open away you go to wherever,
Flowing with the force of life
To heights and depths in the dance
Of truthforce and suffering,
Pouring forth your love and strength
To make this earth a good home.
And I, alas, watch
with sad delight.

War Rant

Beginning of the Iraq war, March 2003
Inspired by the Vagina Monologue performance

Oh geeze, I freeze
War again. "Its no sin…
It's necessary, you hear me,
See what *they* did, and gonna do."
It's the old shoe again, it fits.
"We gotta kill them first,
It's a thirst, can't help it, only way
To stay safe, stay on top."

On top of what,? Of me
Oh geeze, here it comes again…
My mouth is full, its pressing against
My throat, my air, my hair
I can't breathe, 100 billion for war

100 billion, 100 billion, I can't breathe,
I can't cry out "No, NO, STOP! HELP!
RAPE! RAPE! HELP! STOP!"
100 billion, 100 billion for war
"Don't talk—shut up or I'll hurt you more."

100 billion for war, tear down schools,
100 billion, break all the rules
Tear the fabric of society
"Stop! Help!" stop this misery
Lives torn asunder your priority.

No voice. No one hears my cry, my plea
"Please stop world cop,

Cop-out. Cheap Shot!"
I want to shout, shout, make a flood—
"Stop, cop, stop killing, stop spilling innocent blood!"

My blood is boiling,
Oil is spoiling humanity into insanity.
Spoiled soul, spoiled soil, oil spilling
Out of arteries in our homes, our cars, our gadgets
100 billion "Shut up kid." I freeze.
100 billion, trillion, gazillion
I can't breathe.
I'm choking, "Rape!, Rape!"
No one listens, its an old tape.

Oh soul of mine whom I love and guard,
I fear we are lost. Such great cost,
Lost cause, lost reason,
Lost treasures, it's treason.
We're killing to protect what – what?
Why? I sigh. I don't know why.
I can't find the tie between my reality
And the ones with fingers on finality.
Triggers pull, brains blasted, guts torn, lives shattered.
Bang, burst, blast, splatter
Broken pieces of humanity,
Mingled with bones of babies
Born to die, asking "Why?"
Their cries scream into my dreams, and
I can't answer – I swear I'm sorry,
I'm sorry, I'm sorry, I couldn't,
Didn't, couldn't find a way
To say "NO! NO, NO, NO YOU CAN'T!"
Who am I screaming at?

I scream at the night, the blight
Of soul that no longer knows its power.
I scream at the sight of a million dead
While I watch TV and forfeit my sane tomorrow.

Can there be a sane tomorrow?
Can I borrow a hope for change,
A turn-around, a wake up,
A shake-up, a make-up test?
Oh, I know the right thing to say,
Can I have another chance?
Can I say what I mean, really mean to say?
I won't go to war. I won't pay,
I won't believe in war.
I won't kill anymore.

I can't stop writing, writhing,
Hollow holiness cramming air waves,
Filling nooks and crannies of my mind
Till I can't find any memory of kindness.
Any way through blindness
To save those being
Struck down in their homes, in our hearts,
Bones crushed, blood gushed
In the streets of my mind, I can't find
My own sanity anymore.

What else is in store?
What do we do, now the killing's begun
In my name, for our gain—
What do we gain?
Do we win a string of skulls staring into eternity?
Another holocaust to hold,
Burned into our shattered soul?

"Oh Shut up, slut. Unpatriotic."
Idiotic! Insane. I know, I know,
I'm still alive. I know.
100 billion for solar power—
Heal this world in an hour.
Free our soul from oil addiction,
Free our soul from grim perdition.
Free our soul, we are willing.
100 billion to stop the killing.

Give 100 billion to capture the sun.
Give it to children to grow in freedom.
Give it to the millions who want to live,
Leave the oil in the soil, our crimes forgive.

Rape is done. Our soul is won.
I pray, I pray, "Please, everyone.
100 billion for the sun!"
100 billion voices strong,
Ancestors chant in every tongue.

Oh wait, is one still left alive?
Did one survive, who can forgive ?
One, who can ask us why,
Not shy, stand in our face
And find a trace of sanity?
One calling us to forgive who we've become,
Having paid for us our soul's ransom?

The Spoiler

After the BP oil spill, 2009

The oil is coming—unbelievable—
A breach unleashed,
Uncontrollable,
Spewing into the world of water,
Clogging gills, feathers, and marshes,
So many lives battered.
Oil—so convenient—our miracle drug
Gets us high, so high, so fast,
But now no plug—we are aghast that
Oil, once so wonderful, now is the spoiler
Of lives, of livelihoods, of landscape enjoyment.
No one knows how long, how big, how far
The oil will spread
Bringing death in it's path, collective dread
How much loss, so much loss,
Who will pay the cost.
Who will say, who will pray
For a way to make this fair, make it right,
Sanity is swamped, out of sight.
Oil into lungs, death comes.
Oops, sorry, no one cared to pay,
No one stayed the course of human rights,
BP says "Yes, we will" then pays for silence.
Dollars for the recruited clean-up crew
If they won't wear masks, or talk to media, too.
Who has answers
For these growing cancers?
The scientists are turned away –
"We'll do it our way" they say.
Do what? Tires and golf balls? Are they able

To plug up a hole in Mother Nature's naval?
Unknowns turning to bones,
Human error turned to terror,
Unchecked peril from our deal with the devil.
The whole world watching, as scientists keep botching,
Caught in the drama of brokenness,
Can't hold on to the past, the familiar, the comfortableness.
Broken lives, broken wildlife, streams of lies,
Now broken promises, and idle lives,
Idle boats, idle fishermen, idle minds filling with despair,
Who will repair these minds and hearts and lives?
Will generations of partnership with nature survive?
Who will restore balance in nature's classroom?
Anger feels right but doesn't transform.
We send forgiveness into the black hole of our own lives,
Where our bittersweet dependence
on this black drug resides.
This is only the tenth largest spill,
Will we be able to find the will
To change, to learn, to stop this crime?
Oh my God, oh my God,
Will we learn this time?

Oh Say Can You See

After the BP oil spill

Oh say can you see
By the dawn's early light,
Oil spilled on our flag
Stretching far out of sight.
With wars to fuel
While closing schools,
Juggling joblessness and loop holes,
We postpone the turtles' return
To their place of dominance, as our hopes and dreams burn
Up gushes the oil, flames lick the sky,
While the whole world watches
Our swelling black eye.

So we meet our own shadow in the oil slicks on water,
Our greed and injustice for the whole world to ponder.
Gluttons for oil, what gets in our way we kill,
Cast fishermen adrift with generations of skill.
Who will care for the children, the fish, the mammal nation?
Who will care for our moral stagnation?

Come again to the table all who are able,
Find common ground, pass justice around.
Breathe through the not-knowing, how long? How bleak?
Embrace each other, give aid to the weak.
May we rise from these ashes with more wisdom endowed,
Eyes open wide to the choices before us now.
Be the home of the brave, turn the page on the past.
Open our hearts to life's balance at last.
Then will our banner proudly wave,
Our children secure in our care,
Our pride finally saved.

Spiritual Resilience

("There is no time not to love" —Deena Metzger, 2003)

I want to despair.
There is no time not to love.

I want to hate.
There is no time not to love.

I want to scream "No! Stop!"
There is no time not to love.

I want to separate, run away.
There is no time not to love.

I want to deny, to forget, to just be happy.
There is no time not to love.

I want to reject, repel, condemn.
There is no time not to love.

I want to claim a higher moral ground.
There is no time not to love.

I want to give up, just let them kill each other till its done.
There is no time not to love.

I want to declare the death of American civilization.
There is no time not to love.

I want to declare the death of hope for a just humanity.
There is no time not to love.

I want to feel powerful.
There is no time not to love.

I want to be proud of my country.
There is no time not to love.

I want to tell my children it is good to be an American.
There is no time not to love.

I want to be a confident, content, happy human being.
There is no time not to love.

I want to live in the truth of my soul and be free.
There is no time not to love.

Lost Dreams of Easy Times

Soft, juicy blue of berry waiting forever
For two friends to return,
To reach out, and
Touch,
Peel and taste the lost dreams of easy times,
Relax into pine-quiet and remember loving.
Oh haste, waste, the years of
Fervent quest
Away from the breast
Of warm, close holding,
Gentle easiness…
Taste of horror-gloom now,
Can't let it go
Into despair,
I care,
Love the world,
Yet lose myself to me, to you.
Oh soul sister of mine,
The blueberries— ripe, swelling—
Call to us,
"Come play!"
Why have we forsaken each other
For a hungry world
That cannot taste
The sweet fruit?

Mom

So far away
Yet within me, Mom
Screaming your fear, your "NO!"
Daughter—brave,
Believing in my own dreams—
Outgrowing
Mom.

Empty Nest

Who names the cruel spent-ness
That leaves a mother lonely and tired?
Watching dust settle on footprints
Reminiscent of being needed,
When finally we look within for
The truth of the story—our story—
That we poured ourselves out
And became part of the earth
In the doing—
Our souls soar above
The empty nest
Singing of our good nobleness.

Love Embraces Us

When a friend has died

Love calls us into Being.
Love embraces us all our days.
Love blows us a kiss and gives thanks
When we leave.
Love feels the hole left by our departure.
Love weeps for missing us.
Love treasures our memory
And tells our story.
Love cherishes us forever.

Recovery

I love you.
I believe in your wholeness
Even as I see your brokenness.
I am not afraid of your shame or my own,
And I don't need to do anything to change you.
Your journey of healing
Blesses my own imperfection.
Spill the shame out
And let it go.
You are already forgiven.
You are free to
Let good things be your daily bread.
Welcome home to yourself, dear one,
Your fear, disappointment and shame
Will blend with, strengthen and enrich
The unique, radiant beauty of your divine soul.
Welcome home to your innocent child
Who does not fear who she is.
Hold her hand tight.
Never let her go.

Give the World to the Women

International Women's Day, 2006

Time is up for wasting lives,
Telling lies,
And yes-ing spies
While innocents die
And children ask "Why?"
Men stealing elections
With puffed up erections,
Jerking off while the whole world watches,
Marches,
Screams,
Then moves on without them.

We say "Stop the War!"
We say "Stop the squandering of life, and limb,
And peace and possibility!"
We say "No" to killing,
"No" to drafting the poor,
"No" to recruiting our children with myths
And lies about the glory of war.
"No" to building nuclear power plants
And permanent radiation storage.
"No" to accumulating stuff bought cheap with others' lives.
"No" to ….the list is endless.
Oh my soul—how I long to lift my head up and
Be proud of who my people have become.
Oh my soul—Cindy*—Kathy*—Madea*—
Warriors for justice— you cut a path for us.

We are behind and around you.
You give us back our pride and dignity.
We are strong, we are determined.
We are full of rage, and truth,
And determination to have our world.
And we will have it!

(Code Pink leaders Cindy Sheehan, Kathleen Kelly, and Medea Benjamin)

To Listen for the Guidance of Spirit

Communion

Communion—coming together in sacred space—
opening to the Divine in the present moment, I
come, I come. I stand, one hand holding the potent
green drink, the other raised above my head to better
draw down the energy to which I am reaching.

I lift the chalice to my lips. The surface is a swirl
of spinach-green, beet-red, and cauliflower-white
foam. I hesitate. I breathe into this moment
before I drink, to remember the soil, the sun,
the rain, the minerals, the microbes—such a
vast presence gathered in this sacred cup.

I drink this miracle of life. I feel it flowing down the
back of my throat, entering the mystery that is my
body, beginning its long dark journey through channels
thin and wide, until its final passage through each
cell wall into the domain of the life force itself.

Here, in the Temple of All Being, this mighty
elixir will deposit its gifts on the altar of life.
Life giving life to life, and I the witness.

A smile arises as I empty the vessel. The body and
blood of divine presence now lives in every cell of my
body. I am made holy. There is only health in me. I am
washed clean of toxins. My body radiates with the gifts
miraculously released as the juice from garden greens
transforms into my body and blood. I bow in reverence,
stunned by the beauty of this joining—communion.

Living into Love

Come, women, to the womb of the Mother.
Drink from her breast,
Feel her mighty arms enfold you.
Allow her knowing touch to heal you.
Hear her soothing voice singing to you.
See in her face and body the
Reflection of your beauty.
Rise up to meet her call to be a
Daughter of the earth, a healer.
Step onto your path with focus and direction,
Fearless and full of vision.
Sing a love song of joy and thanksgiving to yourself.
Speak your truth to others.
Be known.
Follow your hunches, and
Risk your most daring dream.
Let go of all that holds you back
From giving your gifts to the world.
Give them freely and boldly.
We are waiting.

In the Heart of Spirit

Will we learn in time that we can only
survive by pulling together?

Will we settle our disputes in time, and stop
whatever pushes us down or pulls us apart?

Will we stop the depletion in time of the very
resources—air, water, soil--we need to live?

Will we reverse the urge to greed and privilege in
time to preserve a future for our children?

Will we curb pollution in time, and over-
consumption, and the extremes of poverty and
privilege that enrage the soul of the world?

Will we respect the balance in nature in time, take only what
we truly need, and preserve the rest for future generations?

Will we teach our children in time that true security is in
serving the common good and leaving no one behind?

Will we weave together the threads that sustain the
fabric of life in time—honoring the sacred, respect-
ing Nature's wisdom, conserving resources, and
consecrating our lives to the weaving?

Will we call ourselves one tribe in time, and
choose leaders who build alliances for peace?

Will we sing new songs in time, songs that lift
the weight of inertia, give us strength,, unite us,

and inspire us with vision and perseverance to
make the mighty shift required to survive?

Will we muster the bravery in time to stay the course
of justice, no matter what resistance arises?

Will we let go of yearnings for comfort and ease
in time—and accept that what must be done will
demand more than all that we have to give?

Will we put ourselves in the heart of Spirit in time, and know
that we will be given all we need to accomplish our goals if
we just say "Yes," and keep taking the next step together?

Pilgrim

Pioneer on the path,
Asking questions that pull you into
The future
With just the right balance
Of competence and question,
Willing to be known—
Demanding to be shown,
Quieting, letting go,
Noticing NOW.
Sometimes feeling weak,
Allowing others to lead, and
Mustering the spiritual strength to wait
Until you are ready.
Open up what does not have an answer.
Dwell in mystery.
Cast off obligation.
Birth your vision,
And the will to enact it.
Are you scared? Yes.
Are you awake? Yes.
Are you remembering to breathe? Yes.
Are you willing to be changed by the Life Force? Yes.
Are you willing to freely wait in the not-knowing
Of the yet-to-be-understood? Yes.
Then dance, for you have come
To the center of all that is—
The holy city you seek.
All argument is illusion.
All judgment is illusion.
All power is illusion.
Just dance!

When Change Comes

When Change comes,
I pet my cat,
I breathe and wait.
I wail, resist, complain, rant,
Bemoan, stomp, clatter, shout, then
I roll up in my quilt.
I tell a friend I'm scared.
I wait for guidance.
I look for the lesson to be learned.
I remember the eternal flame glowing
And warming my core.
I search for allies.
I ponder the cycling of birth, death and rebirth
And tell myself "Don't hold on too tight."
I sing the songs of my soul.
I reach out for a hand to steady me.
I reach in for the source of my courage.
I explore possibility.
I give thanks for loving friends who sustain me.
I sit in my powerlessness.
I practice being still.
I choose acceptance to open—truly open—to what is.
Then I discover more about what love really is.
I let go again and again of how I think things should be.
I long for resonance, for reflection of my truth.
I don't die, yet my past does.
I ask: "Why me? What's wrong?" and there is no answer.
I drop down into "the pain" and find home.
I feel humble, not in control,
A pilgrim journeying toward the holy city with no map.
I walk the labyrinth in blind faith.

I listen to birds, wind, friends, teachers, the I Ching sage.
I look at pictures of babies—now grown—
And treasure memories.
I see my reflection in Indra's net.
I trust in the web of life that holds me.
I let change come.

Stopping to Hug a Tree

I stop to hug a tree.
I am silent, still.
My body empties of chronic urgency.
The tree's rough surface presses into my flesh,
Leaving its imprint—like a calling card--for me to see.
I smell a gentle crispness
In the air,
It tickles my throat.
I wait for more,
But all is still.
I suddenly feel silly, caught in the gaze
Of people rushing by.
I am suspended between their world of busyness
And the world of watching, waiting stillness.
Do I want to be here?
I breathe, re-choose my intent, and
Drop back into the stillness.
The tree is waiting—no—
Calling me to come in.
Come in?
Into being with—
Just being with.
I enter the embrace.
No words,
No thoughts,
No need to make anything happen.
The stillness feels strangely restless now,
As if something is stirring,
Yet all agency has melted through my feet
Into the ground.
I am listening now.
We are getting acquainted.

Somehow the tree is in charge, and
I am its willing comrade.
A slight breeze rustles
The tips of the new green leaves.
The tree is hugging me back.

I Am the Love Already with You

I am the love already with you, Sandra. I am the one who waits for you to let go of needing to know—of needing to be sure. I am waiting. It doesn't matter which fork in the road you take, Sandra, I am there before you, beside you, above you, below you, and within you.

You are safe with me. I will never abandon you. I am good company. I will hold your fear with you until it melts into acceptance. I will not push you, nor pull you. Whether you go forward or step back, I am beside you. You cannot lose my love or my attention. I will accompany you through anything. You are free to choose what will make you happy. We will have a good, full, and complete time together. It doesn't matter whether that time is long or short.

You already know this, Sandra. You already know me— the love that will not leave. But you sometimes forget to connect with me. You wander away into your fretting and fuming, determined to go it alone. You lose yourself. Then you remember. You come back—tired—and find that I am already here, waiting patiently for your return.

Relax, unwind, surrender to love, Sandra. Don't miss a moment of your precious being. And don't forget that you also are the love already here for others. They are relying on you, too, even if they—like you— don't trust it or sometimes forget. So let's celebrate this moment when you do remember me, and see if we can walk together all the days of your life. OK?

Got Soul?

The abolitionists said "No," and
Chained themselves to the fence.
The environmentalists say "Yes," and
March for a sustainable world.
The artist follows her brush and
Her paint spreads red blood
Announcing visions of rebirth.
A friend travels hundreds of miles
To visit another in prison.
A mother strings Solstice lights to beckon the night,
A writer opens pen to page and
Speaks to future generations.
A farmer creates a garden where
Bare earth begs for purpose.
A poet fills the page with the "Aha!"
of wondering and wandering.
An activist scurries from forum to forum,
Calling hearts and minds to live justice for all.

Soul pulses through our days,
Through touch,
Through time,
Through imagination,
Through fear and fact,
Through storm destruction,
Through watching innocent people die,
And still it sings to the dawn.

How Many?

How many kisses convince me that I am loveable?
How many bank accounts prove to me my worth?
How many years unwind before I know
That I never grow old?
How many shades of green fill a forest
Bathed in sunlight?

How Do I Know God?

God is the beauty in a carpet from Isfahan,
A statue from Bali, a ring from Nepal,
A shawl from Peru, a scarf of silk from India.
God is the harmony in great
Symphonies serenading my soul.
God is the silence when there is nothing more to say.
God is community gathering, buzzing with
Welcome, stories, play, and vulnerability.
God is my heart beating.
God is hunger in my stomach that tells me I am alive.
God is nature wiggling, borrowing, pressing and roaring
To correct all imbalance.
God is life's force sometimes moving silently,
Sometimes crashing violently about
The business of transformation.
God is the freedom to create, and then to fall, to fail,
And to let go.
God is the compass,
And home
Is everywhere.

Labyrinth

Circle of stones, laid with care, each placed just so to hold an ancient pattern. The pattern speaks through the stones, silent eyes looking at each passer by, wondering if they hear the stones speaking. I step into the entrance. My eyes rest on the first stone on the path. Gray and course, it has tiny specks of black and white minerals embedded on the surface. Who is calling me here? It is the ancestors. Here they are, one by one, as I slowly move onto the path. Each one unique, holding the energy of earth, rain, sun, moon, heat, minerals—all pushed together like the circumstances of one life, into bumps, crevices, shimmering surfaces, sparkles, and clusters of translucence.

Who are these stones, these sentinels of time? They are aunts, uncles, grandparents, great uncles, great grandparents; the women who yielded to the hunt of the sperm and bore the children; the great-grandfathers who crossed oceans and clear-cut new land to feed their families and tend their precious animals. They are the care-free children who grew into adulthood, moved away, and forged new links between family and fortune. I walk slowly, looking at each stone. What era were you? What spirit sang to your soul? Were you satisfied with your life? Did you reap what you sowed? Were you rich, poor, healthy, or happy? Were you bitter, or did you know grace? Did you do what you took birth for? Did you come home to yourself and enjoy the simple things of life?

Perhaps this next stone could be my Great Aunt Edna. She loved birds and flowers. She was effusive in her wild adoration and the joy of their companionship. Next might be my Grandpa Pierre Bontecou, her brother. He loved business, progress, and character (he gave me the Bontecou

Achievement Award named after himself). His wife, Elsie—next in the curving line—filled the home, church and concert hall with Chopin etudes, sitting like a queen at the grand piano that was draped in a black silk shawl, shimmering with elegant fringe. I used to sit on the bench next to her while her fingers flew past my nose. Hearing an etude today puts me right back on that bench next to her.

Moving on, Uncle Ken loved to dance and laugh. Next to him is his wife, Aunt Marie. She was the life of any party (sometimes too raucous for the rest). Now I see Aunt Adrienne, who had flaming, long, red hair (like a calendar pin-up), and a gorgeous smile. Her personality was radiant as a star, riveting attention. Next to her is my Uncle George. He was kind and friendly, easy going.

Stones, stones, some are round, some flat, uneven or smooth. Like the people of the past, each is unique, each holding its space in the sacred pattern of life's spiral into the center of being.
I move on. The stones are beckoning me. My father's sisters were distant, shadowy silhouettes of the Waymer family from St. Louis. Dorothy had a daughter named Susan. I remember watching her dress Susan's hair in a perfect French twist once, wondering what it was like to have a mother like that. But that's all I know of Dorothy except that she died suddenly and far away of a brain tumor. Only murmurs rippled through the family.

That was some time after my father, Sam Waymer, died of cancer when he was 48. I see him next in line. Some stones never get to be old and plump. They are smoother, rounder—like his—less weathered by life. He was sick for six years. No one knew much about cancer in 1959. He was part of experimental treatments. No one talked about it, even after he died. I was just 19, but my whole life changed after that. He is surely one of these stones calling out "Remember me! Remember me!"

Moving on—here is his sister Margaret. She was a talker. She mostly talked out loud to herself about nothing in particular. When I was older, I found some precious nuggets among her ramblings. They were scarce, but once she told me that my father always wore a white linen suit to church on Sundays, and he would iron it himself in the basement every Saturday night. My Dad followed his passion, serving boys and building character. He started Boy Scout troops for a living, moving our family every two years as he pioneered the nation with good deeds, courage and skill. He loved flowers, and our home was always surrounded with gardens.

Curving ever toward the center, my Mom, Sylvia, is the stone closest to him. She lies in her loyal quietness, ever in his shadow, yet surging with the artist touch that painted Grandma Moses murals on our dinning room walls, hooked our family story into rugs for the stairs, volunteered at the hospital, and played tennis weekly until she died one night in her sleep of a heart attack.

Stone after stone, each one occupies its essential niche in the pattern. The labyrinth calls me deeper, back and back I go as I round the way of the labyrinth, weaving inward toward the center. Now the stones have no names, no stories. But one, somewhere far along the path, is an herbalist who wrote a book about natural medicines in Germany during the witch burning times. Was he a witch? Was he a friend to the witches? A genealogist told my grandfather about him. His brave choice to be a voice for the healing power of plants during hot political times brings strength to this labyrinth of my life.

Another, spiraling deeper, is Brahms—also from the genealogist's digging—bringing the passion of music, the blessing of inspiration, the solitude of the artist to this labyrinth design. Perhaps his heart held enough music to reach down the centuries into Elsie's hands. She recorded the artists who came before her all the decades of her life, until her hands were so knurled with arthritis she couldn't play anymore. She couldn't even knit or hold a bridge hand by the end. Amazing, how much her hands expressed her love of life.

Stones, sentinels to the unfolding of Life, sit still as grass grows up where feet have not trod, nestling each one closer to the Mother like a mantle of mercy. Each one was a special child to someone. Each was an old person watching the young grow into their fullness and power. Somewhere among them is the ship captain Bontecou, exploring the coast of China with his fleet of seven ships in 1607.

How is it that his story has come down to my ears in 2000 AD while so many thousand others are lost to the winds and tides? Who were the Waymers when they were still the Weimars of Germany? Who were the Bonetcous when King Louis XV of France threw all the French Huguenots out of his Kingdom in 1790, and they fled as refugees to the new land, first to New York, and then New Rochelle which was named after their home city in France. My grandfather Pierre would eventually settle there as well, and I would attend first and second grade there. What was that journey like? Were the seas high? Were the children frightened and seasick? What possessions were they able to bring with them?

The labyrinth ushers me unexpectedly into the center. I have arrived. Circles and centuries of stones and ancestors surround me. Here I stand, Sandra, a link from these ancestors to the future. Soon I will take my place as a memory, a stone with a story. What will be remembered about her, that one who was born in 1940 and lived through the dawning of a New Age—a radical upheaval of tradition and culture in the 1960s. She braved the high seas of women's liberation. She traveled the world with a passion for freedom. She delighted in watching her three sons grow into manhood and carry the echoes of her courage, vision and caring into another generation. She will be a story that is known for a while, then becomes another silent stone calling out to the next passers by.

Where did this path begin? It is lost to the passing of time. Now, there is only the path and the walking. There is only the voice of the ancestors singing quietly to my soul, "Welcome home." Standing in the center, there is only this moment. Feeling the sun, hearing birds awakening to Spring, I feel the deep presence of the Great Mother who birthed us all, yet never dies herself. She creates the rhythms of death and rebirth. She lays each stone in its place in this great labyrinth of Her heart. Each ancestor seemingly a separate stone, but to Her eyes they are all one labyrinth—a testimony to Her faithfulness, Her love, Her tender care, and Her relishing of life itself—and I am a part of it.

To Bow in Thanksgiving for My Life

We are All One

We are all one,
Sending forth Spirit,
Astride the path,
Alone together.
We are by earth
And sky blessed,
And we are healed
As we let go.
And we give thanks,
Receiving what we need,
Return to love,
Blessed be.

(Music to this chant can be found at www.DenverChantCircles-subscribe@yahoogroups.com)

Bestowing Blessing

Bees buzz from flower to flower,
Drinking in blessing, bestowing blessing,
Carrying pollen on their feet.
Birds sing anthems to me, to us, to all around,
While worms, responding with praise,
Leap into their hungry beaks.
I breathe in—a blessing.
I breathe out—bestowing a blessing,
Flowing from tree to me to tree
To eternity.
The flow goes on, flow on,
The earth, the air, the fire, the water
Return, return, return, return,
Turning ever into me
Out of me
Through me
Above me
Below me
Until there is no me,
Only blessing.

Duet of Praise

Guardian tree,
Standing straight and tall,
Reaching above all the others nearby,
Your stately strength holds ancient knowing.
You watch with silent eyes
That radiate presence.
Now in early morning, we gather near-by
To sing greetings to the Four Directions.
A small bird perches on your top-most branch, and
When we finish our song,
The bird sings back to us.
We all hear it—a duet of praise,
Drawing us into communion.

Now, years on, I see that tree again
In my reverie,
With singing bird
Warbling forth loving presence,
And we still singing back.
Time dissolves into
Connection and
Eternal song.

Ego and Soul Say Goodbye

Goodbye to fame and travel, to art-making
and child-rearing.

Goodbye to datebook and computer, and to measuring
worth by showing up for projects, for friends, for justice.

Goodbye to the watchful eye minding bank account
and other fuels in the various tanks of necessity.

Goodbye to practicing health, always exercising, stretching
into the future, and planning food responsibly.

Goodbye to garden seed-planting, weed-pulling.
and harvesting of grapes, peaches, cabbages, kale
and all the host of garden treasures; to bending,
lifting, carrying, arranging, storing and cooking.

Goodbye to music-making—guitar, piano, voice—
and all the sacred circles raising song to commune
with the Four Directions and beyond.

Goodbye to meditating, fervent self-educating,
and protecting the environment.

Goodbye to anchoring the family as mother and
grandmother through feast and famine.

Goodbye to the artist's eye—always on the lookout—capturing
an exquisite moment in artifact or photo to share with others.

Goodbye to befriending so many who could add
their needs to her always busy-in-motion life.

Goodbye to the writer collecting stories of adventures
that touch the heart, and planting them in books.

Soul's time now—empty boat, needing nothing
more—just time to say goodbye and farewell.

I Greet Spirit

In the end,

I greet Spirit—my companion through it
all—my greatest teacher, vigilant trainer,
and provider of all my lessons,

Holder of the arena in which I have grown,
honed my gifts, nurtured my relationships, and
found my place in the scheme of things.

I face into the Light open-hearted, trusting, and
ready to receive again whatever Spirit has to offer.

I surrender all my expectations, fears, and illusions.

I open to mystery, to join—and be
changed yet again—by Spirit's spiral.

I pour out my praise, my love of life, and my
reverence for the beauty of this world with
its sunsets, stars, birds, fish, four-leggeds,
songbirds, desserts, mountains, rivers, lakes,
oceans, lovers, children, friends—all of it.

I drink in the blessing to have been a
part of this magnificent creation.

I bow in gratitude and grace.

Grandmother Sandra

The ancient surf is rolling now, but you hear it only
for a short while. The birds sing out their presence
to the world and you hear it for just a short while.
The blossoms—so brilliant against the sky—bob
on stem, heavy with color, for just a little while.
You once had a Grandmother, Katie. Her name
was Sandra She breathed, danced, birthed, and
journeyed for just a little while. When she left, her
soul was chocked full of the birdsong, the blossom
scent, and the sound of the surf soothing her soul.

Sandra loved you, Katie. She loved your sparkling
innocence and bubbling beauty. She loved the
arch of your eyebrow, the curl of your eyelash,
the eagerness of your smile, and the gift of your
giggle. First grandchild, you changed her into a
grandmother and blessed her path with joy.

Oh Katie, how she loved you, coming as distant daughter
through her life of sons, your petticoats tossing, your
running feet so rooted in the feminine. She pined to
hold you and stroke your hair, to sing lullabies to your
sleeping ears and tuck the quilt gently under your chin.

For a while the sun rose into Sandra's waiting face.
Prayer on her lips, she searched each dawn for blessing,
for discovery, for the courage to accept what life
would bring without complaint. Oh, she failed—how
she failed. She had a ferocious stubborn nature, very
determined to have its own way. Life had to discipline
her again and again—ah yes, and again, having to
withhold its fullness until she could find it among
the pieces of her days, never in one whole moment.

You had a Grandmother for a while. Her name was Sandra. Her feet walked through many lands of this world in search of jewels in the hearts of God's creation. She listened with sacred curiosity, resting in the hospitality of the Nicaraguan mother, the Nepali innkeeper, the Syrian family, Jordanian, Turkish, German, Egyptian, English, Ugandan, Malawian, Zimbabwian, Mexican—across the hearth—Lebanese, Greek, Spanish, French, Ghanaian—across the table, across the campfire, across the sacred texts, passing food, drink, song, and prayer. Her touch held the touch of so many, her skin and belly blessed by loving touch found everywhere.

Oh Katie, you had a grandmother for a while. Her name was Sandra. She loved with all her being, yet she could not linger long with any one lover. Life was her lover. Not one for hearth and home, she was a wanderer who tasted of many forbidden fruits. Unafraid of the tree of knowledge, she did not give reverence to any one God, but loved them all equally for the power of wisdom and guidance they gave—yet none ever greater than the one inside herself. She left no stone unturned, hungry for adventure, for knowing what life could be, breaking any rule that stood between her and justice.

Oh Katie, you had a Grandmother for a while. Her name was Sandra. She prayed for you every day, that your life would be free and bold—yes BOLD. Could she possibly pass that fire onto you—that burning desire to risk, forfeiting the familiar, the easy, the safe for the greater wisdom of the vulnerable, the lost, the pilgrim? "Look into the shadows, child," she would cry. "Venture around the corner out of sight, away from safety's gaze. Be born of the earth itself, the sky, the sea, the wild animals calling in the night and at dawn. Be born of the fresh spring bursting out of the mountainside. Be born of the wild flowers ablaze in the high meadow. Be born of the smoke curling from solitary hut in a foreign land. Ride a camel across a desert, ride a donkey up a mountain trail, ride a taxi, a subway, a monorail. Ride a ski lift to the top of the world. Ride a tram to the high trail, a train to the border. Ride a bicycle to a friend. Ride a sleigh through winter woodland, a hay wagon through summer full moon. Ride a schooner to far island, a freighter to beyond the horizon. Ride, Katie, ride, ride over the sea to the wilderness of your heart!"

There, just there, when you arrive, tired and dirty and amazed and welcomed by a stranger, there, just there, dear one, you will meet your Grandmother Sandra again. She will glow in the fire of their hearth. She will smile out of their eyes and touch you with weathered, wrinkled hands. She will sing in their shrill ululating, in their melodic love songs, in their tendering lullabies. She will wink at you from exotic blossom where your eyes are compelled to linger. She will beckon you with the sound of the surf calling, calling, calling "Come to the edge of all you can see and know and wade in. Feel the power of the sea sing to the salt in your bones."

Oh Katie, you once had a Grandmother. Her name was Sandra. Can you feel her as you watch the dawn rising? Can you sense her whispering "I love you?" Can you see her up ahead on your path beckoning "This way, this way dear one"? Do your feet want to follow? Do you dare to leave all behind? Come as far as you can, child. You will do it your way, and she knows that. She is the wind. She will blow where she will. And she will always return. Always return.

Oh Katie, you once had a Grandmother.

Her name was Sandra.

Sandra Boston lives in Greenfield, Massachusetts where she has a psychotherapy practice (which includes phone counseling) and offers board and staff training in conscious communication skills. She is also available for motivational speaking engagements. She can be reached by email at bostons111@gmail.com
or by phone at 413-774-5952.

Copies of this book available at
https://www.createspace.com/5918127

Other books by Sandra Boston are

Out of Bounds: Adventures in Transformation, 2014, 312 pages. $14.99

Copies available at
www.createspace.com/5149857

Aiming Your Mind: Strategies and Skills for Conscious Communication, 2005, 150 pages. $18

Aiming Your Mind: Strategies and Skills for Conscious Communication with practice exercises 200 pages. $25

Copies available by contacting the author via e-mail or her website: www.ccitraining.org

www.ingramcontent.com/pod-product-compliance
Lightning Source LLC
Chambersburg PA
CBHW071509040426
42444CB00008B/1560